THE WORLD OF DINOSAURS

ARGENTINOSAURUS

BY REBECCA SABELKO

EPIC

BELLWETHER MEDIA · MINNEAPOLIS, MN

EPIC BOOKS are no ordinary books. They burst with intense action, high-speed heroics, and shadows of the unknown. Are you ready for an Epic adventure?

This edition first published in 2021 by Bellwether Media, Inc.

No part of this publication may be reproduced in whole or in part without written permission of the publisher. For information regarding permission, write to Bellwether Media, Inc., Attention: Permissions Department, 6012 Blue Circle Drive, Minnetonka, MN 55343.

Library of Congress Cataloging-in-Publication Data

LC record for Argentinosaurus available at https://lccn.loc.gov/2020048045

Editor: Betsy Rathburn   Designer: Jeffrey Kollock

Printed in the United States of America, North Mankato, MN.

TABLE OF CONTENTS

THE WORLD OF THE ARGENTINOSAURUS

The Argentinosaurus was one of the largest land animals to ever live! It grew more than 121 feet (37 meters) long.

This dinosaur lived around 95 million years ago during the Late **Cretaceous period**. This was during the **Mesozoic era**.

MAP OF THE WORLD

Late Cretaceous period

NAME GAME

The Argentinosaurus gets its name because its fossils were found in Argentina. Its name means "Argentine lizard."

PRONUNCIATION

ahr-gen-TEEN-oh-SORE-us

WHAT WAS THE ARGENTINOSAURUS?

The Argentinosaurus had four sturdy legs. They held up its heavy body. The dinosaur weighed about 165,347 pounds (75,000 kilograms)!

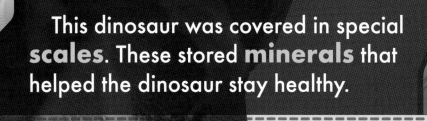

This dinosaur was covered in special **scales**. These stored **minerals** that helped the dinosaur stay healthy.

⚠ GROWING BABIES

A young Argentinosaurus gained around 88 pounds (40 kilograms) each day!

⚠ SIZE CHART

35 feet (10.7 meters)

25 feet (7.6 meters)

15 feet (4.6 meters)

5 feet (1.5 meters)

The Argentinosaurus had a long neck and tail. These helped the dinosaur stay balanced while moving.

It walked very slowly. It only moved around 3 miles (4.8 kilometers) per hour!

DIET AND DEFENSES

The Argentinosaurus was an **herbivore**. It mostly ate leafy plants.

The dinosaur used its long neck to reach food. Its pencil-shaped teeth pulled leaves from branches.

ARGENTINOSAURUS DIET

leafy plants

tree leaves

flowering shrubs

This giant dinosaur had to eat a lot!
It swallowed its food whole. This allowed
the dinosaur to eat more at one time.

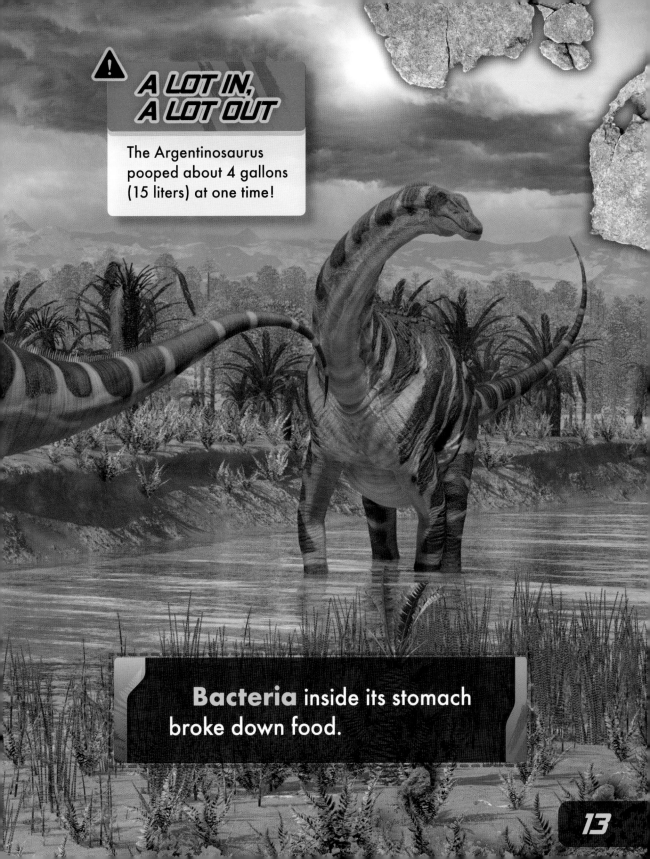

Bacteria inside its stomach broke down food.

The Argentinosaurus was too big for most meat-eaters to take down. But groups of mapusaurus and giganotosaurus may have attacked the dinosaur.

mapusaurus

herd

The Argentinosaurus may have lived in **herds**. These groups helped the dinosaur stay safe.

FOSSILS AND EXTINCTION

Earth began to change during the Late Cretaceous period.

The Argentinosaurus could not survive the changes. The dinosaur went **extinct**.

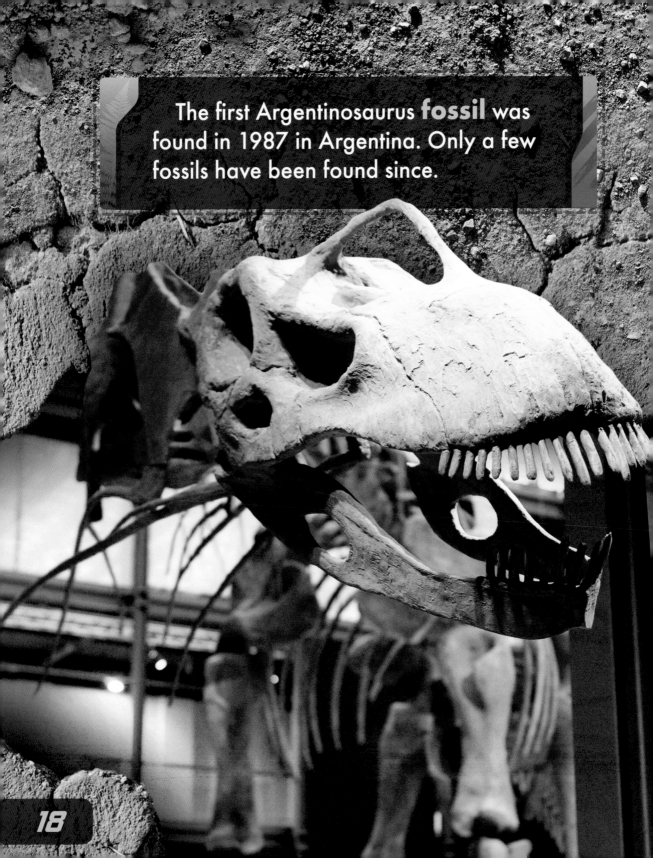

The first Argentinosaurus **fossil** was found in 1987 in Argentina. Only a few fossils have been found since.

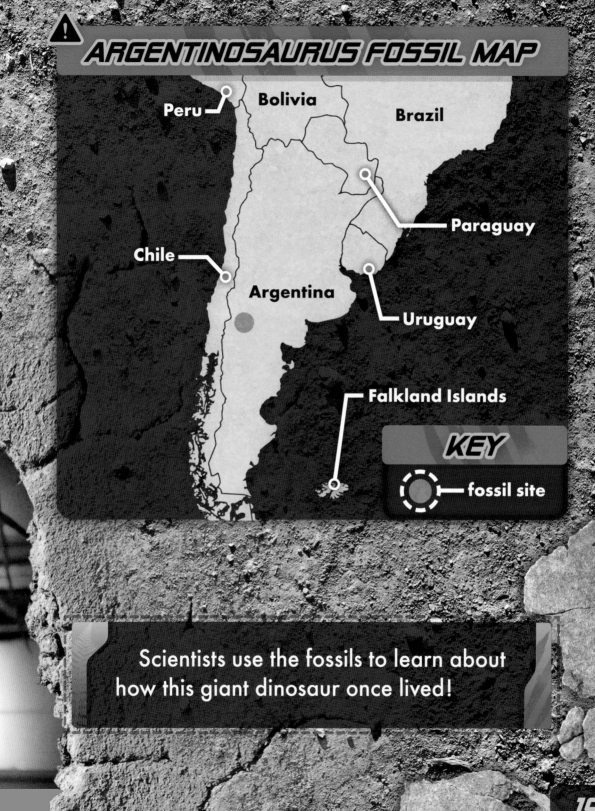

ARGENTINOSAURUS FOSSIL MAP

Peru

Bolivia

Brazil

Paraguay

Chile

Argentina

Uruguay

Falkland Islands

KEY

○ fossil site

Scientists use the fossils to learn about how this giant dinosaur once lived!

GET TO KNOW THE ARGENTINOSAURUS

small head

long neck

HEIGHT more than 26 feet (8 meters) tall at the shoulder

⚠ FIRST FOSSIL FOUND

1987 in Huincul Formation, Argentina

⚠ LOCATION

South America

LENGTH up to 121 feet (37 meters) long

100 million to 66 million years ago during the Late Cretaceous period

Mesozoic era

| Triassic | Jurassic | Cretaceous |

scales

⚠ **FOOD**

leafy plants

tree leaves

long tail

⚠ **FOUND BY**

Guillermo Heredia

⚠ **WEIGHT**

up 165,347 pounds (75,000 kilograms)

🦕 = 🐘🐘🐘🐘🐘 🐘🐘🐘🐘🐘 🐘🐘🐘🐘🐘

GLOSSARY

bacteria—tiny creatures that live inside animals; some bacteria help animals break down food.

Cretaceous period—the last period of the Mesozoic era that occurred between 145 million and 66 million years ago; the Late Cretaceous period began around 100 million years ago.

extinct—no longer living

fossil—the remains of a living thing that lived long ago

herbivore—an animal that only eats plants

herds—groups of dinosaurs that lived and traveled together

Mesozoic era—a time in history in which dinosaurs lived on Earth; the first birds, mammals, and flowering plants appeared on Earth during the Mesozoic era.

minerals—elements found in the earth that animals need to stay healthy

scales—small plates of skin that covered and protected an Argentinosaurus's body

TO LEARN MORE

AT THE LIBRARY

Braun, Eric. *Could You Survive the Cretaceous Period?: An Interactive Prehistoric Adventure*. North Mankato, Minn.: Capstone Press, 2020.

Owen, Ruth. *The Biggest Dinosaurs*. New York, N.Y.: Bearport Publishing, 2019.

Sabelko, Rebecca. *Apatosaurus*. Minneapolis, Minn.: Bellwether Media, 2021.

ON THE WEB

FACTSURFER

Factsurfer.com gives you a safe, fun way to find more information.

1. Go to www.factsurfer.com.

2. Enter "Argentinosaurus" into the search box and click 🔍.

3. Select your book cover to see a list of related content.

INDEX